Copyright

Belfort Sales Secrets & Tricky Tactics: How to Sell like the Wolf of Wall Street

Copyright © 2014

Table of Contents

Introduction

Our life is all about selling whether you like it or not. Obviously, not everything has a monetary value but the value we attach to what we are always selling, be it friendships, businesses ideas, products or services determines whether we will succeed in our endeavors or not. We simply cannot help ourselves because if we present ourselves short of what we really want, nothing good can come out of it. Whether you are approaching your boss for a promotion, selling a product to a prospect or trying to make your friends believe in your ideologies, you are selling. In as much as you may not like sales people, a sales job or simply the name sales, it is pointless to believe that you are not a salesperson of your life, your business, your ideas and everything you want others to believe in.

For any of this to come to pass, good communication skills play an integral part in enabling you to get there; a good product and a good business name isn't just enough to get you a sale. Being the best employee and having your employer's interests at heart won't get you a pay hike. Excellent communication is essential if you are to move your product, idea or service to a prospect. Do you know that good communication and outstanding sales skills is what will differentiate you from everyone else who is trying to sell whatever they believe is the best product in the world?

Do you know that people will only buy from you because they like you, like the product you are selling and like your company? All this happens subconsciously in a prospect's mind when making a sales pitch. Actually, your prospect will have decided to buy from you in the first few seconds of meeting you whether it is across the street, your business premises or over the phone. Do you know that the more of a salesman you are, the more successful you are likely to be in anything you do; plain and simple! In a business setting, how do you think customers come to you? Did someone refer them to you, did they just find your business in the midst of the many, have you met before, did you give them an appointment, or did they find you through the internet? One way or the other, selling is involved. You simply cannot substitute sales for anything else that your business could do to grow; having the best products won't just cut it! You don't need to be running a business per se, all your life involves selling yourself whether for monetary or non monetary consideration.

Now that you know that sales is indispensable in your business or personal life, is it time to get straight to selling? Not so fast, you have to sale right if you are to make every contact with a prospect a deal closing session; no second or subsequent rounds! Mhhh... does it sound close to impossible to be closing deals every time you meet or call prospects? Yes. That's close to impossible if you are an average salesperson with average sales tactics! However, this is a daily routine when you master how to sell like the Wolf of Wall Street; Jordan Belfort! This book seeks to demystify sales strategies that transformed Jordan Belfort from being a nobody salesman to the world's top most paid sales person and motivational speaker charging upwards of $30,000 for a speech! This book isn't about growing you to be a motivational speaker, it is about transforming you to become the salesperson you only dream of becoming once you implement Belfort's Straight Line Selling System, which saw him earn in excess of $50 million a year as a Wall Street Stock Broker. Isn't that someone you want to be like? In simple terms, you will learn how to start selling like the real Wolf of Wall Street through aligning yourself and your team to start learning on the specific elements of the inner game of how to succeed in your business irrespective of the environment. You will also get to learn about the specific techniques and strategies that are necessary to effectively build, manage, promote and grow your business to its best. In a nutshell, the book addresses Belfort's three core elements that probably pull you and your team back from succeeding, four special elements on how to condition your mind in a way that will enable you dominate any business situation and how to use the straight line persuasion technique to make every meeting a deal closing time. Coming from a guy who taught uneducated kids to start closing every deal they were faced with, you can be sure that Belfort's Straight Line Selling System will work irrespective of who you are. You also get to know how to create instant rapport with anyone, anywhere and take full charge of the sales conversation to close all closable deals. Doesn't that sound like something you want to do even in succeeding the business of your personal life? Whatever you do in selling yourself, your company or your products or services, use the ABC rule (Always Be Closing). In simple terms, if you don't get to a closure in a single conversation, count that as a loss! So, let's get straight to it in discovering how to do an impressive opening, an engaging presentation and an undeniable close to get those sales coming to you.

Create An Impression When Meeting Someone New

The opening

Everyone meets so many people each day; some are sales people trying to sell their products and services to you. However, who among those you meet for the first time do you end up remembering their name or where you kept their business card two days later? Can you even recount the experience you had with such people? The difference between those you meet and forget about them and those whose memories last for months or even years is simple; they stood out from the crowd in one way or the other! Remember, the perceptions we have about everyone we meet every day determines whether our subconscious self will consider worth retaining for the long haul. So how do you get to a point of being the guy that your prospects want to meet again? How do you become the guy who closes every other deal in any new encounter? How do you get to a point where you are always closing? The answer lies in three simple strategies namely being sharp, enthusiastic, and authoritative if you are to pass the prospects' mental filters that determine whether to continue listening to you and do something or not. This is what makes an unforgettable opening in any deal and is only meant to be the first 4 seconds of meeting a new prospect. No talking is involved here!

#1. Stand out as the sharpest guy that the prospect has met in a long time

Who doesn't like meeting sharp people? I mean people who challenge you without making you feel uncomfortable or someone who you just connect with little or no effort. In the business of selling, knowing how to implement this inner game strategy will not only create lasting first impressions but also make you create instant rapport with your prospects, which is an essential recipe for closing deals real quick. The more the prospect believes you are sharp, the easier it will be for you to sell anything, anywhere to them.

#2. Stand out as being enthusiastic

Who wants to meet a tired salesperson who is just trying to give their newly made sales pitches a try? Someone who doesn't seem sure about themselves and what they want to achieve in meeting a prospect will probably sell him or herself short. You don't want to fall in the category of "nice try but no" especially in the prospects' mind. As part of the opening, your enthusiasm plays a great role in determining whether the prospect will simply activate all salesman filters or believe you and want to listen to what you have on offer. Remember, all this happens in the first 4 seconds of meeting a new prospect; if you are to close the deal that day, showing how enthusiastic you are will make the prospect want to give you a chance to sell whatever you want to sell. Remember, it doesn't have to be a physical product or a business opportunity; selling yourself to friends, your boss or a potential employer should also involve showing your fiery enthusiasm. Enthusiasm is a critical part in creating instant rapport with your prospects. You don't want prospects getting an impression that you are selling to them because you have to; make them feel as if you love everything about what you are selling and they will probably want to associate with what you have on offer.

#3. Stand out as an authority

When you are meeting new people, you don't want to be like everybody; you want your prospect to believe everything you have to say and offer to them. In this case, you have to know your product inside out, know your industry, your company and everything that pertains to what you are offering if you are to stand out as an authority (expert) in whatever you are offering. Creating such an impression will prepare your prospect to listen to what you have to say (your sales pitch). All this happens in the first four seconds of meeting a new prospect; everything is about the impression that your prospect has of you that will determine whether he or she will want to listen to you or not.

In a nutshell, the opening part is meant to give the prospect the impression that you believe 100% in your product, know what you are talking about, are sharp and that you are an authority figure in whatever you have on offer. In this case, you or your employees (whoever meets clients first) should have all these features if you/they are to close every possible sale. In simple terms, they should look happy, should be smiling even when new clients walk in without their knowledge and should know your business in and out if every probable sale is to be closed. With that, you will definitely see more customers coming to you.

Once you have gotten past the opening stage and made an impression of being sharp, enthusiastic and an authority, you can move straight to the presentation phase. The client should already be focused and ready to listen to your presentation (sales pitch).

The presentation

Your presentation should be focused on three core techniques of inner game of business success namely appearance, mirroring and tonality. Following each of these techniques will get you to a point of closing deals quickly and easily while building and maintaining the needed rapport with your prospects. Here is how these core presentation strategies will influence your ability to make all your conversations deal closing time.

#1. Your appearance matters

Do you know why it is so easy for you to close a deal when you are dressed in a certain way? It is deep rooted in us that we judge people by how they look. Forget about the old adage that you shouldn't judge a book by its cover! In reality, our first impression about anyone starts with how he or she is dressed. Don't kid yourself that this isn't important. Irrespective of what you are selling (yourself or products and services) and how good what you are selling is, learn to dress the part. This doesn't mean being in suits when meeting everyone; you have to understand your audience if you are to make the first impression that will make your prospect feel comfortable being around you and listening to what it is you are selling. Think about it, why do you think the big shots in the Wall Street dress in suits? It is because they know who they are selling to and the perception that their audience usually have of them when they dress in that manner; you will hardly come across any of them dressed in shorts or bikinis! Dress properly for your audience if you want to create and build the rapport you need to close every deal. There is power in the right dressing; for instance, a police officer in plain clothing doesn't command as much authority as one with uniform. Do you know why? The answer is simple; he or she is properly dressed for his audience, which means he commands authority in his or her sphere of influence!

However, you are not just going to do everything right by doing generalizations about your audience. Gathering intelligence should be part of what you do during your presentation phase to ensure that you get to the secret point of business success, which involves talking to the prospect's inner self. The more you know your audience, the more you will understand what they want and the more you can tailor the conversation in a manner that makes you come out as an authority (solution provider) for whatever the prospect wants to achieve. Additionally, the more you equip yourself with in-depth knowledge of your customers, the easier it will be for you to find solutions to all your prospects' queries; you know what that means! They will see you as an authority allowing them to believe everything you say!

#2. Mirroring

Practicing mirroring with your prospect will make him or her feel comfortable being around you. So what really is mirroring? In layman's terms, it means mimicking what your prospect is doing to make them see themselves in you. This isn't about being funny or anything otherwise you may make your prospect feel awkward and as if you are making fun of them; the point is, make it look natural that you are moving with the rhythm and just happen to have a lot in common in the way you react in different situations. Mirroring is one of the ways through which you get a prospect to subconsciously trust you. For instance, if you are all seated during the presentation, take note of your prospect's body language and try to do what he or she is doing; make sure it seems to come natural or unrehearsed otherwise you will come out as disrespectful or less serious. Simply put; mirror but don't get caught!

#3. Tonality

What tone do you use when addressing your prospects? Is it a monotone? Do your employees use the same tones over and over again irrespective of who they are talking to and when they are talking to prospects? Do you know that the best deals are closed when you evoke the power of tonal variation when trying to put different points across? For instance, when emphasizing a point, you don't have to use the same tone you were using when speaking about other stuff; using this tip will not only make your prospect comfortable listening to you, it will also make them understand which key points they should think about in your conversation. You don't have to speak loudly to make an impact; actually do you know that a whisper makes someone feel comfortable and take heed of what you are trying to put across. Do you know why? It is because it is not just the ordinary stuff that people do, which means your prospect will only hear it when he or she is fully attentive! Additionally, it will also make him or her to feel more comfortable; in any case, how many people do you usually whisper to across the street! I bet they are really few or that hardly happens.

Whether you are doing face to face presentations or are a telemarketer speaking to a prospect for the first time, practicing the concept of tonalities will transform you from the average sales person that you are now to a force to reckon with in sales. The point is, start learning how to control voice in different tonalities if you want to keep your prospects on the straight line to closing any deal.

Most importantly, you have to understand what the prospect needs during the presentation phase to avoid selling what the prospect doesn't want. The core purpose of the presentation phase should be simple; to get your prospects to love you, to love your product and to love your company. These are the big three inner game success secrets that will prepare your prospects to the closure even before you can move into closure. When the prospect loves everything about you, he or she will want to be associated with you (subconsciously). Think about it, we have an inner drive to belong somewhere where we get all the needed help we want for our troubles. Offering that solution through these unique presentation strategies will move your prospect to the mindset of wanting to be part of you.

Tip: Try practicing different tonalities when speaking to different prospects to see what works best; it is only through practice that you can tell when to use tonalities in your conversations. The more you practice, the better you become and the easier it becomes to close deals with minimal effort given that you make your prospects want whatever you are selling.

Although you have to build rapport with the prospect, the sales pitch should be entirely focused on the topic, not on relationship or friendship; prospects understand that you are selling so the more you make it clear to them, the lesser the chances that you may not get to the phase of closing the deal.

Before going over to actually closing the deal, let's take a look at real life scenarios that you can use the Straight Line Selling System to close any deal anywhere.

How to get a pay raise

If you want to get a pay raise, proper communication is key if you want get your employer to give you the much needed salary increase. In this case, you are selling yourself; you have to make a good first impression to your employer if you want to close the deal (pay increase). Before you get started, you have to understand the value of your product; in this case, you and the job at hand are the product. You want to link this with the value that you offer to the employer. When you know all that, find a way to strike a rapport with the boss ensuring that they trust you and connect with you in a way that makes it easy to close. Remember the rule that you should always be closing; apply this in getting your boss to agree to everything you have to say. You should also be clear on whatever you want; how much money you want as a pay hike? Don't just beat around the bush on what it is you want; actually, the faster you move from opening to closure, the higher the likelihood that your request for a hike will be approved. For instance, you can say "I would want a pay rise for $XXX because of A, B, C". Be specific on the benefits that your employer will receive from giving you a raise. By this time, you should have gathered enough intelligence on the problems or challenges that the boss is facing hence allowing you to touch the hot buttons where the employer will certainly not want to turn down the offer.

Use the first four seconds to persuade your boss for a pay hike

For starters, you have to make an exceptionally good first impression when you want to discuss the issue of a pay hike with your boss. You can't create that perfect first impression through words; everything happens without you actually uttering a word! Your tonality and body language are some of the things that will probably get your boss into listening mode allowing you to present your grievances seamlessly to someone who has already accepted what it is you are about to say; in this case, you should come off as an authority in your subject matter. Know what you are worth and understand the ins and outs of your job if you want to make a good presentation that your boss will look forward to a closure. Do you know that certain tones are more pleasing to the ear than others? They even get your prospect (in this case your boss) to drop anything else he or she was doing to listen to you.

Build a rapport with your boss first

After getting the attention from your prospect (boss) get them to want to talk to you. In this case, know which questions to ask and in what way you should show you are listening if you want to create the desired instant rapport. For instance, if they are talking softly, lean back and show how you are listening intently while probably nodding after every other pause to make your boss want you to continue with the conversation. Nodding shows the speaker that you understand what he or she is trying to bring out. Actually, it would be a good idea to match the general posture of the person who is talking; this is mirroring. Actually, the more you connect with your audience, the easier it will become to know when you are disconnected hence allowing you to change the tone to reconnect with him or her.

Keep your boss engaged by asking questions

Asking questions tells a lot on whether the person you are speaking to is actually listening. Actually, asking someone questions that seem well thought makes them feel comfortable and safe with regards to the discussion you are having. Whether you are selling yourself or an employer's products or services, asking the right questions to your audience keeps them engaged and allows you to tell when you are disconnecting with your audience hence allowing you to change tone. Actually, you will only know what the other person wants based on the response you get from the questions you are asking in the conversation. You may be wondering about the type of questions to ask.

The best questions to ask

Although you want to know what your boss wants, you don't just ask any question and expect to get answers that will give you an opportunity to offer your solution. You have to know the context in order to understand their beliefs relating to decision making and buying in general. Understand the issues that are making their life hard. One rule of thumb, don't try to solve problems before you can get the whole story! The biggest mistake you can make at this point is to be too quick to offer a solution to what your audience may be experiencing before actually understanding where the real problem is and what the person really wants.

Getting to know people's problems

For you to get to a point of convincing someone to buy whatever you are selling, you should get them to love your product logically (such that they believe they really need it) and emotionally (such that they feel good about having that product). If you get to this level, you are assured that the audience trusts you and connects with you as a sales person. The same applies to talking to your boss about a pay increase. Don't be afraid to ask questions that seem to get your audience to want to talk about the things they are going through. Actually, you can ask more seemingly invasive questions that would make your audience think through their life and their business; this way, you get them to open up to you. If they believe that you are an expert who is there to solve their problems, you will be like a doctor to them trying to diagnose and treat different health conditions.

Sales isn't about taking advantage of people's problems to make a sale; it is about making the person you are selling to see the other side of the problem. Actually, they will want to be associated with you when you seem to listen to their problems and offer solutions to what it is that is troubling them. The more rapport you build with your boss, the more he or she will open up to you and tell you about his or her fears and struggles and how he would want you to be part of the solution for whatever he or she is experiencing. Isn't that a good place to close? Everything seems just like a straight line, from opening through presentation and close.

The Close

The Straight Line Selling System's inner game of business success is all about closing; a conversation is regarded a loss if it never gets to a close. The close is founded on three simple principles which form part of the inner game of business success; know when to shut up, know when to agitate the problem and finally know when to consult. Before we actually discuss these three principles, you have to understand some building blocks for this to be effective.

Understand how to answer questions before they can actually be asked

You need to know the points where your audience will probably object. With this in mind, you can find ways of handling the objections and offer solutions that will make your audience feel comfortable. All these are issues that have to be dealt with during your presentation just to ensure that your prospect has all his or her questions addressed even before they can ask them; does that sound like a good plan? By doing that, you will get them to believe that you actually care.

Learn to stay on topic

Whatever conversation you are having, stay on topic; don't just start talking about something totally different and expect to close the sale. In as much as creating a rapport means making the audience feel comfortable, you don't want to start talking about how your boss's teenage kids are behaving badly when trying to negotiate for a pay hike. Remember, you are there to sell; not to be a friend. In any case, if you want to be friends, there is always next time so find ways of controlling the direction that the conversation is taking and steer it properly.

Going back to how you should close, you need to observe the three important principles of closing.

Know when to shut up

Keep in mind that you don't want to be talking all time to close a sale. Actually, failure to listen is recipe for a failed deal. In this case, you need to have a scripted sales process that will help you say the important things then shut up. It is paramount to have something specific you want to tell your audience during your meeting; in this case, you should include breaks where you give your audience some time to talk. Even if you don't want your prospect to talk, give them some time to think!

Agitate problem at hand

Get your prospect to talk about his or her business and what is frustrating him or her. In simple terms, agitate the prospect's problems if you are to really solve his or her problems. For instance, you could ask leading questions that will make them talk about specific issues of interest.

Consult

Use your persuasion skills to show your prospect how his or her problems could be solved. In essence, you are showing the prospect that there is a way out of the problems he or she is going through. This makes you come out as a problem solver and as an authority in solving whatever problems the prospect seems to be having a hard time solving. Do you know how that ends? It ends with; CAN YOU DO THAT FOR ME?

Essential Success Tips While Using Belfort's Straight Line Selling System

For you to make every closable deal a close, you have to implement certain strategies that will maximize the chances of getting to close phase.

#1. Be different

Don't just be like everyone else who your prospect has met; make an outstanding impression that will make the prospect want to listen to you. You also need to have a unique selling position that will connect with the prospect and transform the presentation phase to a close with ease.

#2. The straight line

If you are selling, be open about it; don't try to be friends with the prospect otherwise you will lose the focus of the conversation. Maintain a straight line approach to selling. Be clear about the open, middle (presentation) and close then get your prospect to follow you throughout the process. In this case, you should take charge of the conversation by deflecting any unrelated questions that the prospect may ask; try to ask questions that will bring the prospect back to the topic.

#3. Create a sense of exclusivity for your audience

Make your prospect believe that you are offering an exclusive deal. Do you know that exclusivity commands a premium price? Making them believe this will make them want to grab the opportunity now. If you want to offer exclusivity, you could offer your products for a limited time, to a certain zip code, neighborhood or product. Whatever way you use to create the exclusivity, make your audience want to grab the opportunity now.

Start scripting your sales encounters

If you are to take charge of every encounter, it is necessary to have a plan. In this case, you need to script your encounter to ensure that you have a clear picture of how everything will unfold.

Something to Ponder About

Do you have a script that outlines how you talk to customers who walk into your premises? Do you have a script outlining how phones are answered in your business? Do you have a script of how you greet customers when they walk into your premises? Every situation where you meet prospects needs to be scripted otherwise it will be close to impossible to make every encounter a deal closing time. Remember, if you don't close, it is a loss! In any case, you should remember that your prospects MUST:

#1. Love you

#2. Love your product

#3. Love your company

The reason you may not be closing is because you are not getting them to do any one of these things. They simply must love all the three things if you are to make any sale any time anywhere!

Here is a summary of the process just to give you a summary of what your sales process should be like.

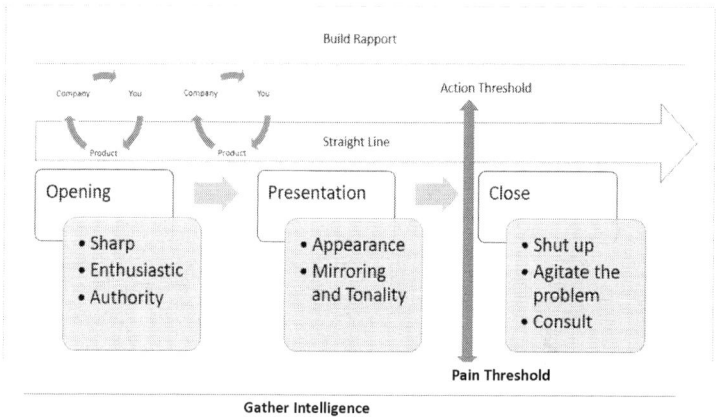

Build Rapport

Company → You → Company → You

Action Threshold

Product   Product   Straight Line

Opening
- Sharp
- Enthusiastic
- Authority

Presentation
- Appearance
- Mirroring and Tonality

Close
- Shut up
- Agitate the problem
- Consult

Pain Threshold

Gather Intelligence

Printed in Great Britain
by Amazon.co.uk, Ltd.,
Marston Gate.